THE
NATIONAL CAPITAL AREA

GONE BUT NOT FORGOTTEN

TARA WEST

—
AMERICA
—
THROUGH
—
TIME

Fonthill Media Inc.
www.fonthillmedia.com
office@fonthillmedia.com

First published 2025
Copyright © Tara West 2025

ISBN 978-1-63499-504-7

Typeset in 10pt on 13pt Sabon
Printed and bound in England

CONTENTS

1

MARYLAND GRAVES

Above left: Benjamin Harris Taylor (July 1, 1888–January 24, 1953). Ben "Old Reliable" Taylor played professional baseball from 1909–1929. Taylor is considered one of the best first basemen in the history of baseball. He was also a longtime manager. In 2006, he was inducted into the Baseball Hall of Fame in Cooperstown, New York.

Above right: Leon Day (October 30, 1916–March 13, 1995). Leon Day was an American professional baseballer who played in the Negro leagues. He was one of the most versatile athletes in the leagues during his time. Day could play every position, with the exception of catcher. Debuting in the Negro leagues in 1934, Leon Day played for the Baltimore Black Sox, Newark Eagles, and the Baltimore Elite Giants. He was inducted into the Puerto Rican Baseball Hall of Fame in 1993, and in the National Baseball Hall of Fame in 1995.

ASPIN HILL CEMETERY

Rags the dog (*c.* 1916–March 6, 1936). Rags was a mixed-breed terrier. He was found and adopted by U.S. Private James Donovan in Paris, France. He would warn soldiers of incoming shells and run messages to the front lines. Rags became the U.S. 1st Infantry Division's dog mascot in World War I. Rags remained the 1st Infantry's mascot until his death in Washington, D.C., on March 22, 1936. Rags was presented with numerous awards and medals.

DULANEY CEMETERY

Arthur James Donovan Jr. (June 5, 1924–August 4, 2013). Arthur Donovan, nicknamed "Art" or "the Bulldog," was professional football player in the NFL. He was a longtime player for the Baltimore Colts. He was inducted into the Professional Football Hall of Fame in 1968.

William Donald Schaefer (November 2, 1921–April 18, 2011). William Schaefer was an American politician who served the people of Maryland for fifty years. He was the forty-fifth mayor of Baltimore, the fifty-eighth governor of Maryland, and the thirty-second comptroller of Maryland.

Above: John Constantine Unitas (May 7, 1933–September 11, 2002). Known as Johnny Unitas by fans, John played quarterback primarily for the Baltimore Colts in the NFL. He played from 1956 to 1973 and is considered to be one of the greatest NFL players of all time.

Left: Spiro Theodore Agnew (November 9, 1918–September 17, 1996). Spiro Agnew was a career politician. He served as the Baltimore County executive. Then, in 1966, he was elected the governor of Maryland. In 1968, he became Richard Nixon's running mate and was sworn in as vice president of the United States on January 20, 1969. As a result of an investigation that uncovered evidence of bribery, kickbacks, and tax evasion during of his time as Baltimore County executive, Spiro Agnew resigned from his position as vice president on October 10, 1973.

GATES OF HEAVEN CEMETERY

Matthew Joseph Thaddeus Stepanek (July 17, 1990–June 22, 2004). Mattie J. T. Stepanek was an American author who published seven bestselling books of poetry and peace essays all before his death at the age of thirteen. He became known as a peace advocate and motivational speaker. He was described by U.S. former President Jimmy Carter as "the most extraordinary person whom I have ever known".

Floyd M. Boring (June 25, 1915–February 1, 2008). Floyd Boring was an American Secret Service agent who served under five U.S. presidents. He was also part of a gunfight that foiled an assassination attempt on former U.S. President Harry S. Truman.

GREEN MOUNT CEMETERY

Arunah Shepherdson (A. S.) Abell (August 10, 1806–April 19, 1888). A. S. Abell was the founder of Baltimore newspaper, *The Sun*.

John Walter Lord Jr. (October 8, 1917–May 19, 2002). Walter Lord was an American author, lawyer, copywriter, and historian. He is best known for his book *A Night to Remember* about the *Titanic*.

Captain Julias Willard (1780–May 6, 1844). Captain Julias Willard fought in the Battle of Baltimore, fighting against the British in 1814.

Elijah Bond (January 23, 1847–April 14, 1921). Elijah Bond was a soldier in the Confederate Army during the Civil War, as well as a lawyer and an inventor. He is best known for his game he patented, the Ouija Board.

Above: Elizabeth Patterson Bonaparte (February 6, 1785–April 4, 1879). Elizabeth Patterson Bonaparte was an American socialite and first wife of Jerome Bonaparte, youngest brother of Napoleon Bonaparte. Napoleon made it known that he was against this marriage and ultimately their marriage was annulled.

Right: Enoch Pratt (September 10, 1808–September 17, 1896). Enoch Pratt was a wealthy American businessman best known for his philanthropic donations to establish the Enoch Pratt Free Library in Baltimore. Enoch Pratt wished to establish a public circulating or lending library that, according to Enoch Pratt, "shall be for all, rich and poor without distinction of race or color, who, when properly accredited, can take out the books if they will handle them carefully and return them."

Etta (Henrietta) Hayne Maddox (January 6, 1860–February 19, 1933). Etta Maddox was the co-founder of the Maryland Woman Suffrage Association in 1894 and the first woman lawyer in the state of Maryland. She had to fight for her right to take the Maryland Bar exam, and having finally won that fight, she earned her license to practice law in 1902.

John Lee Chapman (1811–November 18, 1880). John Chapman served as Mayor Baltimore from 1862 to 1867. He also ran the Maryland Glass Works in Baltimore and served as president of the Western Maryland Railway.

John Wilkes Booth (May 10, 1838–April 26, 1865). John Wilkes Booth was a Confederate sympathizer and the assassin of United States President Abraham Lincoln. Booth was also an actor and a member of the nineteenth-century Booth theatrical family from Maryland.

Johns Hopkins (May 19, 1795–December 24, 1873). John Hopkins was an American merchant, investor, and philanthropist. Hopkins bequeathed large sums of money, thereby founding numerous institutions bearing his name, most notably Johns Hopkins Hospital and Johns Hopkins University.

Thomas Swann (February 3, 1809–July 24, 1883). Thomas Swann was an American lawyer, politician, and the president of the B&O Railroad at the time the railroad reached the Ohio River Valley. He also served as the nineteenth mayor of Baltimore, the governor of Maryland, and a U.S. Representative for the state of Maryland.

Richard Fuller (April 22, 1804–October 20, 1876). Richard Fuller as an American Baptist minister and one of the founders of the Southern Baptist movement.

Left: Issac R. Trimble (May 15, 1802–January 2, 1888). Issac Trimble was a Confederate general in the American Civil War.

Below: Theodore McKeldin (November 20, 1900–August 10, 1974). Theodore McKeldin was a politician who served two terms as the mayor of Baltimore. McKeldin was the governor of Maryland from 1951 to 1959. He oversaw the construction of Friendship Airport, now BWI Thurgood Marshall International Airport. He established interstate 695, 495 Capital beltway, and Rte 50 in his efforts to improve the Maryland highway system.

LOUDON PARK NATIONAL CEMETERY, BALTIMORE, MD

Right: Mary Pickersgill (February 12, 1776–October 4, 1857). Mary Pickersgill was a flag maker. She was asked to make a large flag for Ft. McHenry that could be seen by the British fleet, so she, along with her daughter, Caroline, her nieces, Eliza and Margaret Young, and thirteen-year-old Grace Wisher, who was an indentured servant, made the flag that would fly over Ft. McHenry. This was the flag that inspired Francis Scott Key to write "The Star-Spangled Banner."

Below: Caroline Pickersgill Purdy (1800–1844). Caroline Pickersgill Purdy was the daughter of Mary Pickersgill who, at the age of thirteen, assisted in the making of the flag that flew over Ft. McHenry during the War of 1812.

The American Bonapartes: Jérôme-Napoléon Bonaparte (born Girolamo Buonaparte). He was born on November 15, 1784, in France. He was the youngest brother of Napoleon I and reigned as Jerome Napoleon I, king of Westphalia, between 1807 and 1860. In Germany, he was known as Hieronymus Napoleon. He came to Maryland, fleeing from his brother's anger. He met Elizabeth Patterson, and they were married on December 24, 1803, in Baltimore by Bishop John Carroll, the first Catholic archbishop in the U.S. Jérôme tried to return to Europe with his wife and children, but they had difficulty gaining entrance, and ultimately Jerome abandoned his family and had the marriage annulled in Europe. Elizabeth returned to Baltimore with their son, Jerome. The Maryland General Assembly declared the couple divorced by special decree. Jérôme Napoleon Bonaparte died on June 24, 1860, in France.

Elizabeth Patterson Bonaparte is buried in Green Mount Cemetery in Baltimore.

Jerome Napoleon Bonaparte (July 7, 1805–June 17, 1870). Jerome Napoleon Bonaparte-Patterson was the nephew of Napoleon I, emperor of France.

Right: Susan May Bonaparte (April 2, 1812–September 15, 1881). Sue Bonaparte was an American heiress and the wife of Jerome Napoleon Bonaparte. They had two sons, Jerome Napoleon Bonaparte II (1830–1893) and Charles Joseph Bonaparte (1851–1893).

Below: Elijah Cummings (January 18, 1951–October 17, 2019). Elijah Cummings was an American politician who served in the Maryland House of Delegates from 1983 to 1996. Then he served in the U.S. House of Representatives for Maryland's seventh congressional district from 1996 until his death in 2019. He will be remembered for his years of public service and civil rights advocacy.

MOUNT GILBOA AME CHURCH CEMETERY, OELLA, MARYLAND

Benjamin Banneker (November 9, 1731–October 19, 1806). Benjamin Banneker was born to once-enslaved African American parents. Banneker had no formal education and was largely self-taught. He was a naturalist, mathematician, astronomer, surveyor, farmer, and author. Among his many accomplishments, he worked with Major Andrew Ellicott, surveying and establishing the original borders for the District of Columbia.

MOUNT OLIVET CEMETERY, FREDERICK MARYLAND

Barbara Fritchie (December 3, 1766–December 18, 1862). Barbara, whose last name is sometimes spelled Frietchie, was a Unionist during the Civil War. Poet John Greenleaf Whittier wrote a poem telling a story of how Barbara Fritchie held a Union flag out her window as Confederate soldiers marched through town. Most of the evidence indicates this is likely a fictitious story, however, it has become local folklore.

Bertha Trail (1864–1940). Bertha and her sister, Florence, were suffragists who worked hard to win the vote for women. Bertha was elected president of the Frederick County Republican Club in 1920, where she worked diligently on the registration of new women voters.

Children of the Civil War: This monument is to honor the children who served on both sides during the Civil War. Common roles for children would include serving as orderlies, drummers, horse tenders, dispatchers, and cabin boys.

Claire McCardell (May 24, 1905–March 22, 1958). Claire McCardell was an American fashion designer. She is known for her ready-to-wear clothing, and American sportswear was her hallmark.

Confederate Row contains the remains of 311 soldiers. Mount Olivet Cemetery also has a mass grave containing 408 unknown Confederate soldiers who died in the nearby Battle of Monocacy on July 9, 1864. Many other confederate soldiers who died on or near other nearby battlefields were also placed at Mount Olivet Cemetery.

Francis Scott Key (August 1, 1779–January 11, 1843). Francis Scott Key was an American author, lawyer, and amateur poet. He is best known as the author of the poem, "The Star-Spangled Banner," which was later turned into a song and is now the national anthem of the USA. The poem was written as he observed the bombardment of Fort McHenry in 1814, during the War of 1812.

Above: Mary Tayloe Lloyd Key (May 26, 1784–May 18, 1859). Mary Key is the wife of Francis Scott Key. This was the original burial site at Mount Olivet for Francis Scott Key and his wife, Mary Tayloe Lloyd Key. They now reside in a crypt beneath the Francis Scott Key Memorial near the entrance of the cemetery.

Left: Harriet Hemings Heckman (February 6, 1801–February 26, 1870). Harriet Hemings Heckman is the daughter of Sally Hemings and Thomas Jefferson.

Dr. Phillip Thomas (June 11, 1747–April 25, 1815). Thomas was a physician and loyal patriot during the Revolutionary War.

John and Jane Hanson National Memorial: John Hanson (April 3, 1715–November 15, 1783) and Jane Hanson (September 17, 1728–1812). John Hanson served as a Maryland delegate, was a delegate to the second Continental Congress, and became the first president of the United States under the Articles of Confederation. His actual title was "President of the United States in Congress Assembled." He served in that office from November 5, 1781 to November 4, 1782. President Hanson also established the first Treasury Department, the first secretary of war, and the first Foreign Affairs Department. He died while visiting Oxen Hill Manor, the plantation of his nephew. John Hanson, and later his wife, were buried on this plantation. However, as years went by, the land where they had been buried was redeveloped and the bodies and crypts were lost. On June 25, 2016, a monument was completed to memorialize John and Jane Hanson and their contributions to the nation.

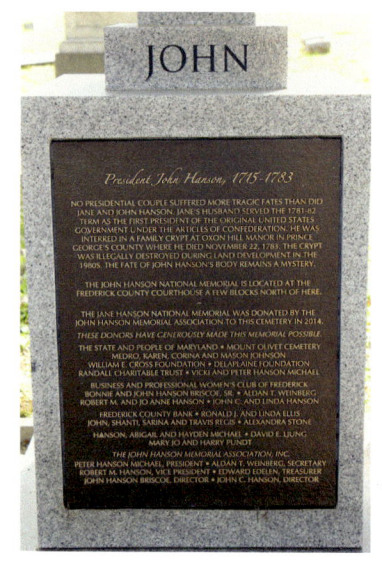

Right: Judge Edward S. Deplaine (October 6, 1893–May 21,1989). Judge Deplaine authored several biographies, including *The Life and Times: Francis Scott Key* and *John Phillip Sousa and the National Anthem.*

Below: Key Memorial Chapel.

Memorial to Soldiers of the Civil War.

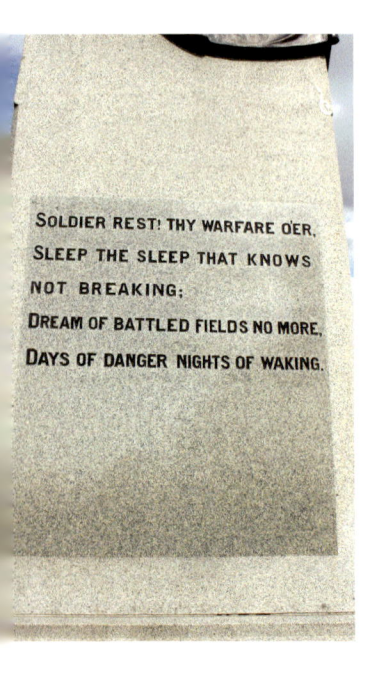

SOLDIER REST! THY WARFARE O'ER,
SLEEP THE SLEEP THAT KNOWS
NOT BREAKING;
DREAM OF BATTLED FIELDS NO MORE,
DAYS OF DANGER NIGHTS OF WAKING.

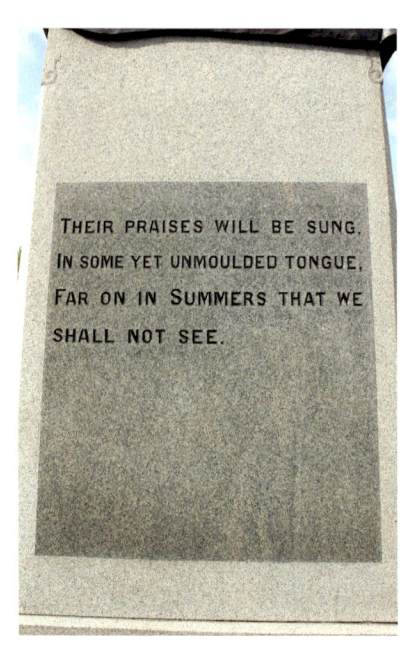

THEIR PRAISES WILL BE SUNG,
IN SOME YET UNMOULDED TONGUE,
FAR ON IN SUMMERS THAT WE
SHALL NOT SEE.

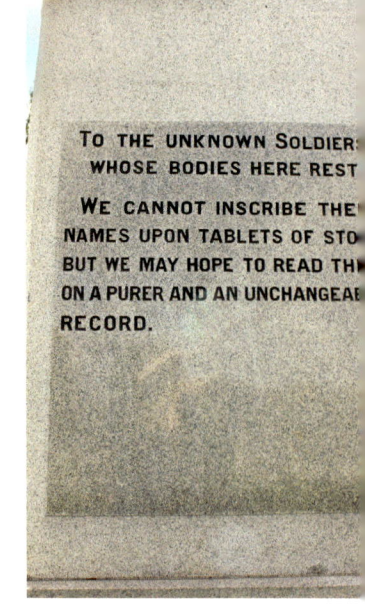

TO THE UNKNOWN SOLDIER
WHOSE BODIES HERE REST

WE CANNOT INSCRIBE THE
NAMES UPON TABLETS OF STO
BUT WE MAY HOPE TO READ TH
ON A PURER AND AN UNCHANGEAE
RECORD.

John Ross Key and Anne Charleton Key, parents of Francis Scott Key.

Richard Potts (July 19, 1753–November 26, 1808). Richard Potts was an American politician who served in a variety of capacities, including a U.S. Continental Congressman, U.S. senator, and a delegate in the Maryland House of Delegates.

Thomas Johnson (November 4, 1732–October 25, 1819). Thomas Johnson was the first elected governor of the state of Maryland.

PARKLAWN MEMORIAL PARKS AND MENORAH GARDENS

Rachel Louise Carson (May 27, 1909–April 14, 1964). She was an author, environmental activist, and educator. She wrote many articles and books about marine life and the poisoning of the environment. She is best known for her 1962 book *Silent Spring*, which revealed the dangers of the pesticide industry and the damage it was doing to wildlife. She has been called the "mother of the modern environmental movement." Her work is credited as being the driving force behind the creation of the Environmental Protection Agency.

PROSPECT HILL CEMETERY, TOWSON MD

Harris Glenn Milstead (October 19, 1945–March 7, 1988). Harris Milstead was best known by his stage name, Divine. Milstead was an American actor, drag queen, and singer. Friend and filmmaker John Waters gave him the name "Divine" and the tagline: "The most beautiful woman in the world … almost."

ROCKVILLE CEMETERY

Walter Perry Johnson (November 6, 1887–December 10, 1946). Walter Johnson was a professional baseball player and manager, donning the nicknames "Barney" and "The Big Train." He was a pitcher for the Washington Senators, then later worked as a manager for the Senators. He finished his career as a manager for the Cleveland Indians, retiring in 1935. He held many records and is still generally regarded as one of the greatest pitchers in the history of baseball.

Rosa Bonheuer Cemetery in Elkridge, Maryland

In 1935, the Rosa Bonheur Memorial Park was founded in Elkridge, Maryland, as one of the world's first pet cemeteries. In 1979, the decision was made to allow owners to be buried next to their pets. The cemetery's namesake, Rosa Bonheuer, was a French painter and sculptor, best known for her paintings of animals.

Left: Gypsy Queen (unknown–October 29, 1936). Gypsy Queen was the horse of Sergeant Frank M. Heath, U.S. Army World War I veteran. He and queen traveled 11,356 miles on the longest trail ever traveled by one horse under saddle, covering each of the then forty-eight states of the Union. They started at the zero milestone in Washington, D.C., on April 1, 1925, and ended at the same point on November 4, 1927. Queen died for the benefit of science on October 29, 1936.

Below: A Pigeon Named Pete (1919–1944). Pete became the unofficial mascot of South Baltimore, beloved of local kids, neighbors, and police officers. Pete was cared for by a young girl, Muriel (Jones) Meyers, from 1919 until Pete's death in 1944.

SAINT JOHN THE EVANGELIST CATHOLIC CHURCH CEMETERY

Above left: Daniel Carroll (July 22, 1730–May 7, 1796). Carroll was an American politician and plantation owner from Maryland and one of the Founding Fathers of the United States. He supported the American Revolution, served in the Continental Congress, and was a delegate to the 1787 Constitutional Convention in Philadelphia. Carroll was one of five men to have signed both the Articles of Confederation and the Constitution.

Above right: The Carroll Family Historic Chapel (Replica). Eleanor Darnell Carroll had this chapel built for her son, John Carroll, who later became Archbishop Carroll. John Carroll was the first Catholic bishop in Maryland and in the United States.

St. Mary's Catholic Cemetery Rockville MD

Francis Scott Key Fitzgerald (September 24, 1896–December 21, 1940). F. Scott Fitzgerald was an American novelist, essayist, and short story writer and is considered one of the greatest American writers of the twentieth century.

St. Mary's Catholic Church in Bryantown, MD

Dr. Samuel Alexander Mudd (December 20, 1833–January 10, 1883). Dr. Mudd was an American physician and a tobacco farmer in Southern Maryland. Dr. Mudd was accused of, and later imprisoned for, conspiring with John Wilkes Booth regarding the assassination of Abraham Lincoln. However, definitive proof of this crime has never fully been reconciled.

TRINITY MEMORIAL GARDENS AND MAUSOLEUM, WALDORF MD

Chuck Brown (August 22, 1936–May 16, 2012). Chuck Brown was an American musician known as the godfather of Go-Go music.

UNITED STATES NAVAL ACADEMY CEMETERY

John Sidney McCain III (August 29, 1936–August 25, 2018). John McCain was a pilot in the U.S. Navy. He was shot down over Hanoi and held as a prisoner of war by the North Vietnamese for over five years, during which time he was tortured and placed in solitary confinement until he was finally released in 1973. He was highly decorated for his courage and valor. He continued to serve his country as a U.S. senator and a U.S. representative for the state of Arizona.

WESTMINSTER HALL

Edgar Allen Poe (January 19, 1809–October 7, 1849). Poe was an American author, poet, and literary critic. He is best known for his poetry and short stories, especially those that were considered to be macabre or Gothic fiction. He is considered the inventor of the detective fiction genre and contributed a great deal to the genre of science fiction.

2
WASHINGTON, D.C., CEMETERIES

CONGRESSIONAL CEMETERY

The Cenotaphs: There are 171 cenotaphs here that honor members of Congress who died in office. Though the term cenotaph means "empty tomb," several of these cenotaphs do serve as the final resting place for many U.S. congressmen.

Anne Royall (June 11, 1769–October 1, 1854). Anne Royall was a writer, newspaper editor, and is considered by some to be the first professional woman journalist in the U.S.

Thomas Hale Boggs (February 15, 1914–disappeared October 16, 1972, declared dead December 29, 1972). Thomas Boggs practiced law before entering into the political arena and served in the U.S. House of Representatives from 1941 to 1943 and again from 1946 to 1972 for the state of Louisiana. He was a member of the Warren Commission, which investigated President John F. Kennedy's assassination. On October 16, 1972, Boggs, who was House majority leader, was flying from Anchorage to Juneau with Alaska Representative Nick Begich when their plane disappeared without a trace. Despite an intense search, neither the plane nor its occupants, Thomas Boggs, Nick Begich, Begich's aide Russ Brown, and pilot Don Jonz, were found. A cenotaph was placed for Thomas Boggs at Congressional Cemetery in 1981.

Mary Martha Corinne Morrison Claiborne "Cokie" Roberts (1943–2019). Cokie Roberts was an ABC News journalist and daughter of Thomas Hale Boggs.

Edward Streeter (August 1, 1891–March 31, 1976). Edward Streeter is an American novelist, best known for his novel *Father of the Bride*. Though he is buried in Forest Lawn Cemetery in New York, this bench resides at Congressional Cemetery in Washington, D.C., to honor his memory and literary contributions.

Opposite page: Elbridge Thomas Gerry (July 17, 1744–November 23, 1814). He was one of the Founding Fathers of the U.S. He had a host of careers including a merchant, politician, diplomat, governor of Massachusetts, and vice president of the U.S. under President James Madison. He was one of the signers of the Declaration of Independence. He was vice president from 1813 until his death on November 23, 1814. While governor, new electoral districts were being created and it was noted that the redistricting was highly partisan, and this is where we get the term "gerrymandering."

Left: William Trimble (April 4, 1786–December 13, 1821). William Trimble was a lieutenant colonel in the U.S. Army. He was a lawyer and a politician in the Democratic-Republican party. He served two years as a U.S. senator from Ohio until his death in 1821.

Below: Mathew Brady (*c.* 1822–January 15, 1896). Mathew Brady was an American photographer remembered as the "father of photojournalism." He is one of the earliest and most famous photographers in American history. He is best known for his photographs taken during the Civil War. He photographed many public figures, including Edgar Allen Poe, Walt Whitman, Susan B. Anthony, Clara Barton, Frederick Douglass, and every U.S. president from John Quincy Adams to William McKinley, with the exception of William Henry Harrison because he passed away so soon after taking office.

Robert Mills (August 12, 1781–March 3, 1855). Robert Mills was an architect known for having designed many churches and public buildings. Among his most famous designs are the Washington Monument, located in Baltimore Maryland, and the better-known Washington Monument that stands on the Mall in Washington, D.C.

Thomas Stephen Foley (March 6, 1929–October 18, 2013). Thomas Foley was the Speaker of the U.S. House of Representatives from 1989 until 1995.

Thomas Phillip "Tip" O'Neill Jr. (December 9, 1912–January 5, 1994). Tip O'Neill was an American politician from Massachusetts and served as the speaker of the U.S. House of Representatives from 1977 to 1987.

Athena Tacha and Richard E. Spear. This headstone or marker is an example of a couple who have not yet passed away but have selected their plot and designed their own headstone monument.

Above: John Edgar Hoover (January 1, 1895–May 2, 1972). J. Edgar Hoover was the last director of the Bureau of Investigation (BOI) and the first director of the Federal Bureau of Investigation (FBI). He served under eight U.S. presidents for a total of forty-eight years, leading the BOI and the FBI.

John Philip Sousa (November 6, 1854–March 6, 1932). John Philip Sousa was an American composer and conductor known primarily for American military marches. He is known as "The March King" or the "American March King." Sousa is best known for his marches "The Stars and Stripes Forever," "Semper Fidelis," "The Liberty Bell," "The Thunderer," and "The Washington Post."

Marion Barry (March 6, 1936–November 23, 2014). Marion Barry served four terms as mayor of Washington, D.C. He was both an influential and controversial D.C. politician. He was an advocate of D.C. home rule and a civil rights leader. Marion Barry proclaimed himself to be an advocate for the poor and dispossessed. Despite controversy surrounding accusations of corruption and drug possession, Marion Barry remained beloved by many D.C. residents.

Dr. William Boyd (1820–February 13, 1884). Dr. William Boyd was one of many abolitionists who served as conductors on the underground railroad.

The Public Vault. This vault served to hold bodies until they could be buried. This vault held the remains of U.S. presidents John Quincy Adams, Zachary Taylor, and William Henry Harrison, as well as First Lady Dolley Madison.

Push-Ma-Ta-Ha (*c*. 1760–December 24, 1824). Push-Ma-Ta-Ha was a Choctaw warrior, diplomat, and chief. He served with Andrew Jackson in the Battle of New Orleans during the War of 1812. He died while in Washington, D.C, seeking payments for debts owed to his nation by the U.S. government.

THE WASHINGTON NATIONAL CATHEDRAL

HELEN KELLER
1880 – 1968
AND HER LIFELONG COMPANION
ANNE SULLIVAN MACY
1866 – 1936
ARE INTERRED IN THE COLUMBARIUM
BEHIND THIS CHAPEL

Above: Helen Keller (June 27, 1880–June 1, 1968). Helen Keller was an American author, an advocate for those with disabilities, and a political activist. Keller became the first deaf and blind person in the U.S. to earn a Bachelor of Arts degree. She was named one of *Time* magazine's "100 Most Important People of the 20th Century."

Anne Sullivan (April 14, 1866–October 20, 1936). Anne Sullivan was an American teacher known for being the teacher and lifelong companion of Helen Keller. Sullivan was partially blind due to an eye disease she contracted as a small child. She graduated from the Perkins School for the Blind. At the age of twenty, she became Helen Keller's teacher.

Opposite above: Matthew Wayne Shepard (December 1, 1976–October 12, 1998). Matthew Shepard was an American student at the University of Wyoming. He was beaten, tortured, and left to die because he was openly gay. He died six days later at a hospital in Fort Collins, Colorado. Shepard's murder brought international attention to hate crimes and the need for hate crime legislation. In 2009, the Matthew Shepard and James Byrd Jr. Hate Crime Prevention Act was signed into law.

Opposite below: Woodrow Wilson (December 28, 1856–February 3, 1924). Woodrow Wilson was a member of the Democratic Party and an American politician, who served as the governor of New Jersey and then as the twenty-eighth president of the U.S. from 1913 to 1921.

ROCK CREEK PARK CEMETERY

Abraham Baldwin (November 22, 1754–March 4, 1807). Abraham Baldwin was one of the Founding Fathers who signed the U.S. Constitution.

Alice Lee Roosevelt Longworth (February 12, 1884–February 20, 1980). Alice Longworth was the eldest daughter of U.S. President Theodore Roosevelt and Alice Hathaway Lee Roosevelt. She married Representative Nicholas Longworth III, a Republican Party leader and thirty-eighth Speaker of the House.

Charles Israel Corby (June 29, 1879–February 13, 1926). Charles Corby and his brother, William, were baking innovators. Their contributions modernized the baking industry. They standardized and mechanized the bread-making process as they perfected the machinery and processes used in factory bread making. Their bakery became famous for its "Mother's Bread," which it advertised as being "pure as mother made it." "Mother's Bread" later became known as Wonder Bread.

Colonel George Bomford (1780–March 25, 1848). Colonel Bomford was a distinguished U.S. Army officer, an inventor, and a designer of weapons and defensive installations. He served as the second chief of ordnance for the U.S. Army Ordnance Corps.

Colonel Edward Brook Lee (October 23, 1892–September 21, 1984). Colonel Lee was a member of the Maryland House of Delegates, the secretary of state for Maryland, and the comptroller of Maryland. He also served in the Maryland National Guard during World War I.

Eugene Charles Allen (July 14, 1919–March 31, 2010). Eugene Allen was a waiter and butler who worked for the U.S. government at the White House for thirty-four years. He retired as the head butler of the White House in 1986. Allen's life inspired the 2013 film *The Butler*.

George of McGovern (July 19, 1922–October 21, 2012). George McGovern was an American historian and South Dakota politician. He served as a U.S. representative and a three-term U.S. senator. In 1972, McGovern was the presidential nominee for the Democratic Pary

George Washington Riggs (July 4, 1813–August 24, 1881). George Riggs was an American businessman, banker, and co-founder of Corcoran and Riggs Bank. Later it became Riggs Bank. He was known as "The President's Banker." His firm secured many of the loans the Federal government needed for the Mexican-American War. He was a trustee of the Corcoran Gallery of Art and the Peabody Education Fund.

Henry Langsburgh (February 2, 1869–November 29, 1925). Henry Langsburgh was a respected and well-liked D.C resident and the vice president of Langsburgh & Bro Department store in Washington, D.C.

Charles Francis Jenkins (August 22, 1867–June 6, 1934). Charles Jenkins was an American engineer who was credited as a pioneer of early cinema and one of the inventors of the television. He used mechanical rather than electronic technologies. He was the founder of Charles Jenkins Laboratories which, in 1928, was granted the first commercial television license in the U.S. This was the beginning of the Jenkins Television Corporation. Over 400 patents were issued to Jenkins, many for his inventions related to motion pictures and television.

Colonel John James Abert (September 17, 1788–January 27, 1863). John Abert was a colonel in the U.S. Army. He was the head of the Corps of Topographical Engineers for thirty-two years. He played a crucial role in the mapping of the American West.

Above: Julius Garfinckel (November 5, 1872–November 5, 1936). Julius Garfinckel was a prominent American business executive and philanthropist. He was the founder of Julius Garfinckel's and Company, a Washington, D.C., area department store chain. The department store was later called Garfinckel's and was a prominent a D.C. area department store from 1905 until the company filed for bankruptcy in 1990.

Left: Henry (February 16, 1838–March 27, 1918) and Marian Clover Hooper Adams (September 13, 1843–December 6, 1885). Marion was an American socialite in the Washington, D.C., area. Henry was an American historian and a descendent of two U.S. presidents. He served as an ambassador to the U.K. during Lincoln's administration.

Mary Lockwood (October 24, 1831–1922). Mary Lockwood was one of the founders of the Daughters of the American Revolution. She was a friend and advisor to women's rights activists Elizabeth Cady Stanton and Susan B. Anthony. She authored books and newspapers articles about women's rights.

Montgomery Blair (May 10, 1813–July 27, 1883). Montgomery Blair was an American politician and lawyer. He served as the postmaster-general under the Lincoln administration from 1861–1864.

Rosalie Poe (December 1810–July 21, 1874). Rosalie Poe was an American poet and the sister of Edgar Allan Poe.

Upton Beall Sinclair Jr. (September 20, 1878–November 25, 1968). Upton Sinclair was an American writer and political activist. He wrote numerous books and other works in several genres. In 1904, Sinclair spent several weeks in disguise, working undercover in Chicago's meatpacking plants researching for his novel *The Jungle*. Originally published serially in 1905, then as a novel in 1906, *The Jungle* exposed the horrible conditions in the plants and the struggles of poor immigrants. Sinclair won the Pulitzer Prize for Fiction in 1943 for *Dragon's Teeth*.

3

VIRGINIA CEMETERIES

ARLINGTON NATIONAL CEMETERY

Arguably among the world's most renowned cemeteries. It is the final resting place to former presidents, politicians, explorers, celebrities, and more than 400,000 soldiers, sailors, marines, and airmen, all who are heroes who served our country with valor. Because of the vast number of people buried at Arlington National Cemetery, this book highlights just a relative few of the most notable.

Pentagon Group Burial Marker. This is the site of a mass grave containing the recovered remains of the people who were killed on September 11, 2001, at the Pentagon and on American Airlines Flight 77. A funeral service was held on September 12, 2002, at the Memorial Amphitheater in Arlington National Cemetery.

Audie Murphy (June 20, 1924–May 28, 1971). Audie Murphy was an American soldier, actor, and songwriter. He is one of the most decorated combat soldiers of World War II.

The Space Shuttle *Challenger* Memorial. This memorial honors the seven crew members who were killed on January 28, 1986, when the Space Shuttle *Challenger* exploded seventy-three seconds after takeoff.

The Space Shuttle *Columbia* Memorial. This memorial honors the seven crew members killed on February 1, 2003, when the shuttle burst into flames upon re-entering earth's atmosphere.

The Buffalo Soldiers Centennial Memorial (July 1, 1898–July 1, 1998). This memorial honors the Buffalo soldiers who fought in the Spanish-American War alongside Teddy Roosevelt's Rough Riders.

The Tomb of the Civil War Unknowns. This original Tomb of the Unknown Soldier is the final resting spot of 2,111 unidentified soldiers whose bones were recovered from fields of Bull Run and along the route of the Rappahannock.

Above: Tomb of the Unknown Soldier. In 1921, this tomb was established to serve as a place to honor and remember those military servicemen who died but whose remains could not be identified.

Left: General Colin Luther Powell (April 5, 1937–October 18, 2021). General Colin Powell was a soldier for thirty-five years, rising to the rank of four-star general. He was highly decorated soldier, statesman, and diplomat. He served as the U.S. national security advisor from 1987–1989. He was the chairman of the joint chiefs of staff from 1989–1993. He served as secretary of state from 2001–2005.

Edward (Ted) Kennedy (February 22, 1932–August 25, 2009). Ted Kennedy was an American lawyer and politician. He served as a U.S. senator from Massachusetts for nearly forty-seven years. He was the brother of President John. F. Kennedy and U.S. Senator Robert F. Kennedy.

Admiral Hyman G. Rickover (December 24, 1899–July 8, 1986). Admiral Rickover was known as "the father of the nuclear navy." He ended his service as a four-star admiral. He is considered by many to be the one of the most important and influential military officers who has ever served in the U.S. Navy.

General Omar Bradley (February 12, 1893–April 8, 1981). General Bradley was a senior officer of the U.S. Army during and after World War II. He was the first chairman of the joint chiefs of staff.

Opposite page: Iranian Rescue Mission Memorial. This memorial honors the U.S. service members who were killed during the attempted hostage rescue mission that took place a midst of the Iranian Revolution of 1979.

Pan Am Flight 103 Memorial (Lockerbie Memorial Cairn). This memorial commemorates the 270 lives lost in the terrorist bombing of Pan American Airlines Flight 103 on December 21, 1988, over Lockerbie, Scotland. The cairn was a gift from the people of Scotland. It is made of 270 blocks of red Scottish sandstone, one for each of the people who were killed. A cairn is a traditional Scottish monument honoring the dead. On December 21, 1988, Flight 103 was *en route* from Frankfurt, Germany, to New York via London's Heathrow Airport. Just after leaving London at 7:02 p.m., the plane exploded, leaving a debris field over the city of Lockerbie. Of the 270 killed, eleven were in Lockerbie, killed by debris. The 259 passengers and crew included citizens of twenty-one countries. Among them were 190 Americans.

The Rough Riders. As it states on the monument, this was erected in 1906, "In memory of the deceased members of the 1st U.S. Volunteer Cavalry, Spanish-American War, erected by the members and friends of the regiment, 1906."

General Philip Kearney Jr. (June 1, 1815–September 1, 1862). General Kearney served in the U.S. Army as well as in French Emperor Napoleon III's Imperial Guard during the Battle of Solferino. He was an honored leader in the U.S. military during the Mexican-American War and the American Civil War. He was the first U.S. citizen to be awarded the French *Légion d'honneur*. He was killed in the Battle of Chantilly on September 1, 1862.

Opposite page: John Herschel Glenn Jr. (July 18, 1921–December 8, 2016). John Glenn had a long resume which included serving as an aviator in the U.S. Marine Corps, an engineer, astronaut, businessman, and politician. He was the third American in space, and the first American to orbit the Earth. He served as a U.S. senator for Ohio from 1974 until 1999. In 1998, he flew into space again at the age of seventy-seven.

Pierre L'Enfant (August 2, 1754–June 14, 1825). Pierre L'Enfant was born in Paris, France. He left France to enlist in the American Revolution on the side of the colonists. He served with George Washington at the Battle of Valley Forge. In 1791, he drafted the basic plan for the city of Washington, D.C.

Robert Peary (May 6, 1856–February 20, 1920). Robert Peary was an American explorer and a U.S. Navy officer who made several expeditions to the Arctic region in the late nineteenth and early twentieth centuries. In April 1909, Peary lead an expedition and claimed to be the first to have reached the North Pole.

Matthew Henson (August 8, 1866–March 9, 1955). Matthew Henson was an African American explorer. He is best known for accompanying Robert Peary on his voyages to the Arctic. They claimed to have reached the North Pole or the "Farthest Point North" on April 6, 1909. Henson claimed to have been the first of their party to reach the North Pole.

William Howard Taft (September 15, 1857–March 8, 1930). William Taft was the twenty-seventh president of the U.S., serving from 1909 until 1913. In 1921, Taft was appointed by President Harding to be chief justice of the U.S. He was the only person to have held both offices. He was the first U.S. president and Supreme Court justice to be buried in Arlington National Cemetery.

Above: Oliver Wendell Holmes (March 8, 1841–March 6, 1935). Oliver Holmes was an associate justice of the U.S. Supreme Court from 1902 until 1932 when he retired at the age of ninety. Holmes is one of the most commonly cited Supreme Court justices and considered to be among the most influential American judges in history.

Right: Joan Ruth Bader Ginsburg (March 15, 1933–September 18, 2020). Ruth Bader Ginsburg, also known as RBG, was an American lawyer and an associate justice of the U.S. Supreme Court. She served from 1993 until her death in 2020. Ginsburg was the second woman to have served on the Supreme Court and the first Jewish woman to have done so.

Above: Thoroughgood "Thurgood" Marshall (July 2, 1908–January 24, 1993). Thurgood Marshall was an American civil rights lawyer and an associate justice of the U.S. Supreme Court from 1967–1991. He was the first African American Supreme Court justice. Prior to serving on the high court, he used his talents as at attorney to fight for civil rights and end racial segregation in the American public schools.

Left: Medgar Wiley Evers (July 2, 1925–June 12, 1963). Medgar Evers was decorated for his service as a U.S. Army combat soldier during World War II. As a civil rights leader, he fought to end segregation in public spaces and to ensure the voting rights for African Americans. He was assassinated by Byron De La Beckwith on June 12, 1963.

Walter Reed (September 13, 1851–November 22, 1902). Walter Reed was a physician in the U.S. Army. In 1901, he and his team confirmed the theory, posed by Dr. Carlos Finlay, that yellow fever is transmitted by a particular mosquito species rather than by direct contact. This ultimately led to the new fields of epidemiology and biomedicine.

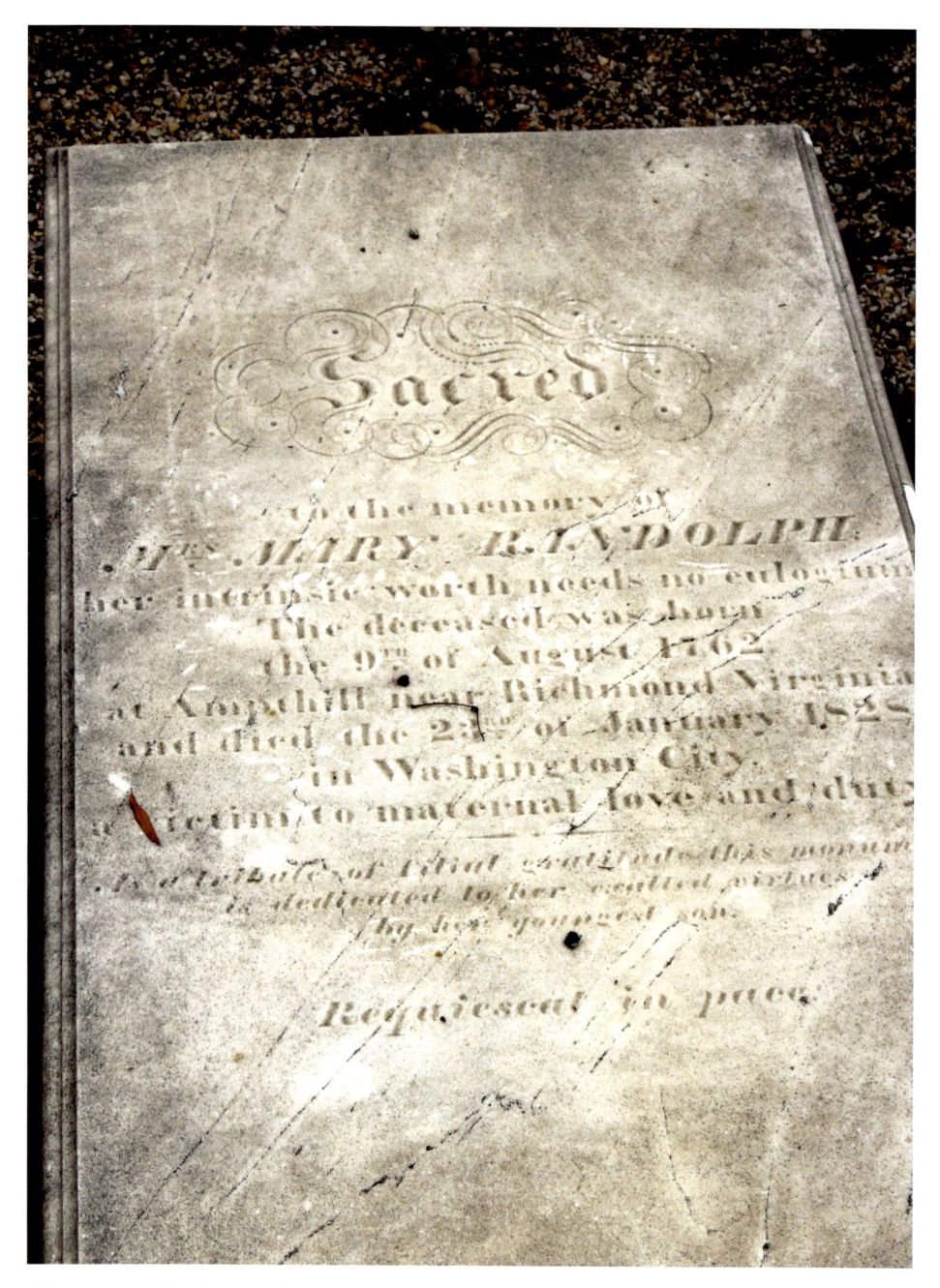

Mary Randolph (August 9, 1762–January 23, 1828). Mary Randolph was an American author of the cookbook *The Virginia House-Wife*. It was an early housekeeping and cookbook which included many local Virginia ingredients. She was the first person known to be buried at what is now Arlington National Cemetery. Prior to becoming a national cemetery, it was the home of her cousin, George Washington Parke Custis, the father of Mary Custis, wife of Robert E. Lee. Mary Randolph's grave is a short distance from the Arlington house, once the home of George Washington Parke Custis.

MOUNT VERNON, VIRGINIA

George Washington (February 22, 1732–December 14, 1799). George Washington had a long resume which included farmer, surveyor, military officer, politician, and statesman. He is best known as one of America's Founding Fathers and the "Father of the Nation." In 1787, he served as the president of the Constitutional Convention whereby the Constitution of the United States was drafted and ratified. He served as the first president of the United States from 1789 until 1797. He is the only U.S. president never to have lived in the White House.

Martha Dandridge Custis Washington (June 2, 1731–May 22, 1802). In 1750, Martha Dandridge married Daniel Parke Cusits, one of the wealthiest men in the Virginia colony. Custis died seven years later in 1757. In 1759, the widow remarried George Washington. When her husband took office as president of the U.S., the title of "first lady" had not yet been established and Martha was referred to as Lady Washington.

Slave Burial Area

"Near [George Washington's] tomb you see the burying place of his slaves containing 150 graves." - Visitor to Mount Vernon, 1833

Many African Americans - freed and enslaved - who worked at Mount Vernon from the 1750s into the 19th century are buried near here, according to early visitor accounts, oral tradition, an 1855 map, and confirmed by a multi-year archaeological survey. Among them is William Lee, George Washington's personal servant during the Revolutionary War, who was granted freedom and an annuity in Washington's will. West Ford (1784-1863), a formerly enslaved man who was hired by the Washington family in the 19th century, is believed to be buried here. The Mount Vernon Ladies Association sought Ford's advice in the early restoration of the estate. Today a memorial stands at the center of the burial area, serving as a testament to the hundreds of enslaved people who labored on Mount Vernon's grounds and lay in unmarked graves.

The Slave Memorial stands adjacent to the Mount Vernon Ladies' Association's 1929 marker. This marks the site of the 200-year-old cemetery.

Opposite page: Slave Memorial at Mount Vernon. This gray, truncated granite column was designed by students from the architectural school at Howard University. Its design represents "life unfinished." It was dedicated and opened to the public on September 21, 1983.

SOURCES

Findagrave.com
wikipedia.com
mountolivethistory.com
congressionalcemetery.org
greenmountcemetery.com
ArlingtonCemetery.mil
nps.gov3*